THE TEACHER
SELF-CARE
MANUAL

THE TEACHER SELF-CARE MANUAL

Simple Strategies for Stressed Teachers

PATRICE PALMER

Alphabet Publishing
1204 Main Street #172
Branford, CT 06405 USA

info@alphabetpublishingbooks.com
www.alphabetpublishingbooks.com

ISBN:978-1-948492-31-7 (paperback)
978-1-948492-44-7 (ebook)

Discounts on class sets and bulk orders available upon inquiry.

*To Andrew - thank you for helping me learn
what is truly important in life.*

With love, Mom

*To Ray - your ability to see in me what I haven't
seen has got me to where I am today.*

With deepest gratitude, pp

INTRODUCTION

"Self-care is not selfish. You cannot serve from an empty vessel."
~Eleanor Brownn

WHEN I first read the quote above, I felt like Eleanor was speaking directly to me using a nice soft, caring teacher voice. Unfortunately, by that time I had left a career that I loved because of professional burnout. It's not like I woke up one morning burned out; it was a long, slow burn. I felt guilty because I felt like I wasn't strong enough or "superwoman" enough to do it all.

As teachers, we give so much to our students. Our career is a labour of love and we pride ourselves on our ability to care and help others. Teaching is a profession that requires giving of oneself to make a difference for students. The ability to empathize with our students often takes place in an environment with little or no job security while meeting the demands of exhausting workloads. The chronic use of empathy and depletion of emotional resources are strongly associated with emotional exhaustion and/or professional burnout (Maslach, Schaufeli & Leiter, 2001). For example, students may have faced trauma; in the case of ESL students, they may come from war zones or refugee camps. Sometimes the teacher is the only trusted person in that student's life. It is difficult not to care for our students when they confide in us or ask for help.

Another problem in higher education is the rise of precarious and insecure work. Part-time positions rarely include health benefits or pay for sick days and that can lead to harmful health effects. At one point, I had seven part-time contracts at one college in order have the equivalent of a "full-time" salary. These "jobs" ranged from teaching, developing curriculum, managing ESL programs, and recruiting students for specific courses. Precarious work is a growing trend especially for ESL and post-secondary faculty in Canada and other parts of the world. Precarious workers are three times more likely to rate their health as less than good, so the promotion of well-being through access to health benefits is needed along with more stable employment (Access Alliance, n.d.). Emotional depletion, burnout, and high attrition in the profession may be costly for the educational system—both financially and academically (Klusmann, Richter, & Lüdtke, 2016). There is considerable research that further supports this:

- Teachers experience as much stress as paramedics and police officers. (Johnson, 2005)
- Teaching was ranked as the number one most stressful job in the UK in a comparative study of stressful occupations. (Johnson, 2005)
- Teachers are among those professionals with the highest levels of job stress and burnout across many countries. (Stoeber & Renner, 2008)
- Teachers can be involved in 1,000 interpersonal connections in a day (Holmes, 2005). All that contact can be wearing.
- 40% of teachers in US schools leave their jobs within first five years (CPRE, 2014). Increased legislative and administrative regulations, as well as raised education standards contribute to stress, particularly when introduced with few professional development opportunities, planning time, support, or resources (Action & Glasgow, 2015, Spilt, Koomen & Thijs, 2011, Curry, 2012).

WHAT IS TEACHER WELL-BEING?

Key Definitions

Teacher Well-Being—There has been a significant increase in scholarly research related to well-being. Even though teacher well-being has proven difficult to define, here is one definition that I like:

> Teacher well-being includes a sense of personal professional fulfilment, satisfaction, purposefulness, and happiness, constructed in collaboration with colleagues and students (Soini, Pyhalto & Piertarinen, 2010).

Generally speaking, the research agrees on two things:

1. If teachers can model positive well-being strategies, this will have a positive influence on student well-being, and;

2. teacher well-being is critical for whole school well-being and for students. (McCallum & Price, 2010)

Here are some other definitions of key terms:

Self-care—skills and strategies used to maintain personal, familial, emotional, and spiritual needs while attending to the needs and demands of others (Newell & MacNeil, 2016).

Emotional exhaustion—depleted by the chronic needs, demands, and expectations of students and organizations

Depersonalization—the negative, cynical, or detached responses, such as "I don't care."

Secondary traumatic stress—natural emotions resulting from knowing about a traumatizing event

Meaning burnout—when the meaning and the purpose for the work is gone, but caring is still intact

Burning out—progressive state occurring over time with contributing factors related to the individual, the populations served, and the organization

Professional burnout—physical, emotional, psychological, and spiritual exhaustion (Skovholt & Trotter-Mathison, 2016)

Why is Teacher Well-being Important?

There is a growing interest in the area of student well-being, but the health and well-being of all school staff is important. This means that everyone must flourish, including teachers, administrators, and all staff. However, when we look at a stressful occupation like teaching, healthier teachers have fewer sick days and greater satisfaction. Research studies suggest that learning happens best when teachers and their students are well. But the added benefit is that as teachers flourish, relationships with students, colleagues and the larger community become more positive (Cherkowski & Walker, 2018). Therefore, the learning and working environment is sustaining for all when teachers increase their well-being and flourish through self-care practices.

What Self-Care Is and Isn't

First of all, self-care is not an indulgence. It is an essential component of prevention of exhaustion and/or professional burnout. It is not something "extra" or "nice to do if you have the time" (Barnett, Johnston & Hillard, 2006). In addition, research studies suggest that self-care practices are strongly associated with building emotional resilience—the ability to bounce back or react appropriately when life gets tough—in helping professionals such as teachers. (Higher

Education Academy Research Briefing, 2013). I thought I was a super-teacher and super-mother and didn't need to balance life and work, to slow down, or to take care of myself. Self-care is always important BUT at times of personal crisis or excessive stress, it is even more important. I learned this the hard way.

It is not about making a choice to care for others or for ourselves, but making the choice to attend to our needs and the needs of others. If someone is stranded at the side of the road because their car ran out of gas, do you empty your tank for them? Definitely not.

Initially self-care was thought to be the sole responsibility of teachers, but as Cherkowski and Walker (2018) argue, it is a personal, interpersonal, and organizational responsibility. In addition, Cherkowski and Walker firmly believe that the well-being of teachers, students, and all staff is essential for all schools. They do not believe that teachers should wait until their organizations pay attention to well-being. I agree that even though our organizations may not embrace the importance of self-care, it is imperative that we look after ourselves. Without self-care, teachers are at risk of emotional exhaustion, compassion fatigue, and professional burnout. This can impact teacher recruitment, retention, turnover, and satisfaction.

How Do We Learn Self-Care?

When we start a teacher training program, there are books and resources to teach various subjects, skills, and ages, and levels, but there is no manual for teachers to learn how to take care of themselves or why self-care is essential in the work that we do. It's like taking driving lessons, getting a license, and buying a nice car but then having no idea how to maintain that valuable vehicle. We know that without regular and proper maintenance, that vehicle is not going to last.

Most teachers are planners—from mapping out careers, planning lessons, activities, assessments to improving and developing our skills through ongoing professional development—but neglectful of physical, mental, and emotional health. Self-care is the refueling of the tank—without it, we just can't move, just like a vehicle on empty cannot.

Although I have now left the teaching profession after a 23-year career, I have a soft spot for teachers given my own experience with professional burnout in 2015. I wouldn't want what happened to me to happen to other teachers. To be honest, if someone had asked me at any time during my career what were my self-care practices, I wouldn't have understood the question. Self-care was not part of my vocabulary! I know now that burnout can be prevented with self-care strategies so the purpose of this book is to encourage you to learn and apply simple self-care strategies that work for you as a busy, often stressed teacher.

To prepare for this book, I read several books on teacher self-care and books for a general audience on the same topic. I was lucky to discover the wonderful work of Fran Warren, an educator in the United States and the brains behind the Teacher Self-Care conferences, and have now become a presenter at some of these conferences. In the past few years, I have tried to synthesize what I feel is important to know. But I've also tried to be concise. One book on self-care I read was more than 200 pages! I don't know any teacher who has time to read a 200-page book!

What is the best approach to self-care? We need to find what works for each of us individually. I think it's unrealistic to provide a self-care plan in this book and insist that it is the only way. What I do provide is evidence that supports why teacher self-care is necessary, and how I adopted new mindsets and healthy habits that work for me. I provide some ideas from teachers and at the end of the book, there are a series of questions that can be used for a "book club" style professional development event or just for discussion in the lunch room. I have also included a self-care assessment tool, and some simple activities based on the science of positive psychology that increase well-being.

Teachers are busy people and my goal in this book is to encourage you to make yourself a priority by adapting simple self-care strategies. We must talk about the stress associated with our careers, find ways to be well and stay well, and encourage those around us to follow suit. This book will serve as your self-care manual and a start for you to design your own self-care roadmap.

My Personal Story of Professional Burnout

Many teachers have asked me about my own experience with burnout, how and when it happened, and how I ended up back in the classroom in 2017. When I left in 2015, I told my colleagues that I was "retiring" because I didn't notice that what I was feeling was professional burnout. Deep down, I felt ashamed and weak that I wasn't able to "do it all". It wasn't until 18 months later, when I returned to the college and a colleague remarked how rested I looked, that I heard myself say "I took time off because I was burned out."

The process was a slow unravelling. Reflecting back at that time, there was a lot going on. But I never thought to slow down or do less. In the two-year period before I burned out, I went through a separation and subsequent divorce, my mother died suddenly, and my teenage son was diagnosed with type 1 diabetes. As a single parent, I took on as much work as I could to make ends meet. I had been working at a community college stringing together part-time contracts that had to be renewed every four months. At one point, I had six contracts that included teaching, managing language programs, hiring teachers and recruiting students. And to top it off, I was completing my Master of Education degree part-time in another city! Finally, I hit a brick wall and after working as an ESL instructor for 20 years, I left thinking that was the end of my teaching career—a career that I had loved. It's not like I woke up one morning burned out—it was a long, slow and painful burn like holding onto a rope in a game of tug-of-war where you can feel your hands slipping down the rope. Despite the pain and burn, you keep holding on until you slide off and collapse in a heap on the ground.

The Road Back

I used to substitute teach occasionally for my good teacher friend Nancy who works in a community-based ESL program for new immigrants (a much more relaxed environment than the college system I had been teaching in for the past 9 years). In the fall of 2017, Nancy asked if I would substitute teach for her. I thought about it for a day or two and said yes, assuming that it was for one day, which was the usual request. Wasn't I surprised to learn that it was for 5 weeks?! I knew that I had to do things differently if I was to return to my career, sustain it, and avoid burning out again. I had been studying positive psychology, or the science of human flourishing and well-being, while I was at home. This emerging science investigates the qualities, attitudes, and practices that enable us to thrive, flourish, and increase our well-being. Positive psychology is the fastest growing area of psychology, which is no surprise to me. There are hundreds of evidence-based interventions or actionable tips that we can use to increase our well-being. So I started to put them into practice. Some of those interventions will be discussed later in the **New Habits** section.

THE REWARDS AND HAZARDS OF TEACHING

THE WORK that we do gives us an opportunity to teach, guide, and advise others. These are the joys, rewards, and gifts of our teaching practice and provide us with a sense of satisfaction. I'm sure you feel a sense of pride when you tell people you are a teacher—I do! However, we need to be aware of yellow lights and hazard signs.

The Yellow Light

Before I got behind the wheel of a car, I bought a manual with the rules and signs of the road. It would have been dangerous to get behind a car and drive without this knowledge. We can't neglect road signs, just like we can't neglect "emotional signs" of exhaustion.

When I give presentations on teacher self-care, I use an image of a traffic light. When we see a yellow traffic light, we automatically slow down. So how can we train ourselves to slow down when we need to take a break? As educators, it's important for us to be aware of the warning signs of burnout such as fatigue, mood swings, depression, and loss of empathy.

In my own case, I was physically and mentally exhausted, and had an "I don't care" attitude, but I did not associate it with the process of burning out. I just thought I was irritable and exhausted because of personal issues in my life. I should have clued in though when I yelled at several people in my department for moving a few boxes near my desk. I felt impatient with students (which had never happened before) and stopped caring about my career. But I didn't put two and two together. The worst incident was that I had a falling out with a good teacher friend, whom I had known well for 5 years. Sadly, our friendship ended due to my refusal to meet and talk things out. I didn't have the energy or will to deal with it. I strongly encourage teachers to watch for warning signs in yourself and in your colleagues.

Dr. Christine Maslach has conducted extensive research in the area of burnout and has designed a survey for educators called the Maslach Burnout Inventory. You can take it online at https://www.mindgarden.com/316-mbi-educators-survey. It's affordable to take one test, but you may want to talk to your administrator or school and see if they will pay for a group of teachers to take the test. The test takes about 10-15 minutes and asks you to rate how often you feel emotionally drained or feel indifferent toward the students, for example. I strongly urge you to take the test as a pre-emptive measure.

Warning signs can help you make changes before it is too late as in my case. I believe that one of the reasons why I did not recognize my burning out was because I didn't know anything the signs or behaviours. If someone would have told me that I would leave a job that I described for many years as "the best job in the world", I wouldn't have believed it. I regret that I didn't know the signs and therefore didn't take any measures to change what was going on in my life.

What I learned about returning to the classroom is that I matter and taking care of myself is a priority. I believe it is all about balance too. In hindsight, I was one of those who was too busy driving from place to place to stop and fill that gas tank as it hovered at empty.

I understand how important it is for teachers to take care of themselves. We need to be able to give ourselves permission to rest, relax, and connect with friends and family. I have made a point of telling younger teachers about my own experience to help them make healthy decisions about marking and lesson preparation. Years ago, I was at my son's basketball game but I wasn't watching because I was marking papers. He noticed what I was doing (most likely because my head was down for the whole game). On the way home in the car, he said, "Mom, you never watched me play at all tonight." I could hear the disappointment in his voice. If you ask me today if I remember his comment, I do. If you ask me if I remember what I was marking that night, I don't. Which was more important? In hindsight, I wasn't present and regret that time lost.

Hazards

Hazards are conditions that can accelerate our burning out. Despite the joys and rewards, teaching is a difficult and stressful job.

I've listed some of the hazards that we should be aware of as a teacher. A hazard is anything that can cause danger or create a problem. We use our car hazard lights to warn others that you are a temporary hazard and some of the hazards listed below can be temporary. For example, you may be given a new grade or level to teach in the future, which would remove that hazard. You may have a very large class one semester but fewer students in the next semester. The key here is to realize that any or a combination of conditions can create unhealthy work environments for us. And this list is by no means comprehensive.

Hazards from students

- low motivation
- students who failed are repeating the course/grade
- high level of needs, such as trauma
- large classes
- multi-level classes

Hazards from your own behaviour

- inability to say no
- no set boundaries
- boredom or meaning burnout
- little or no support
- perfectionism
- unrealistic workload

Hazards from your environment

- continuous or late enrollment of students (common in ESL classes)
- negative colleagues
- organizational bureaucracy
- ineffective leadershipprecarious work
- multiple jobs at multiple schools
- no health benefits or sick days for part-time/contract faculty

Caring: the Ultimate Hazard

When you think of the best teacher you know, what adjective comes to mind? If you said caring, then you are in agreement with most students who were surveyed by the Varkey Foundation. In fact, this

Canadian study suggests that nine in ten Canadians see teachers as caring which is the second only to Finland. (Varkey Foundation, 2018). There is a downside to this though. A participant at one of my workshops explained it like this: "The care that we give to our students is so often lost on our family and friends. My family notices how much time I spend at work and try to shine a light on my burning out trajectory."

I do believe that caring too much can be a hazard, but not caring can be a problem too. Caring is an essential quality as teachers. However, it must be strongly guarded throughout our careers (Skovholt & D'Rozario, 2000).

It is the cycle of caring that eventually takes it toll. Have you ever thought of the cycle of caring as a teacher? Think about the numbers of students who enter your class or course, are nurtured for weeks or months, and then leave. Sometimes we know why they leave, but in the case of teaching adult ESL learners, they may just stop coming to class.

I had a student about 15 years ago from Sri Lanka. She came to ESL class every day. And then one day, she just stopped coming. I didn't think much of it because sometimes students move or attend another program. Her husband showed up at lunch hour on a Wednesday to tell us that they were being deported on Friday. She said that his wife was too upset to come to class and say good-bye. We spent the rest of the afternoon in tears, unable to control our emotions.

I never talked to anyone at the time about what happened, but this event has stayed with me until today. Even now when I recall this story in teacher self-care workshops, I get emotional. I know many teachers have faced similar events with their own students. This extreme event may not happen frequently in our careers but we are affected by everything that happens to our students.

Now imagine in a 10- or 20-year career, how many students we care about. The endless cycle of caring is what separates the work that we do as teachers with other professions, and why self-care is critical.

Making It All Work

Do the best you can until you know better. Then when you know better, do better. ~Maya Angelou

Does this sound familiar?

a. Have you ever felt that you needed to mark all the test papers in a night so you could return them the next day?

b. Have you said no to social events because you had to plan lessons?

c. Have you stayed up late searching for just the right reading text, clip art, or lesson idea?

d. Have you ever told your children (or significant people in your life) that you were too busy to spend time with them?

When I ask teachers these questions, they usually laugh. Many of us will be able to answer yes. Where do these mindsets come from? I believe that there are hidden messages that promote the notion of self-sacrifice vs. self-care. Most teachers have a mindset of working hard to the point of denying our needs or putting ourselves first. One teacher told me that she was saying yes to an overwhelming workload because she wants to be considered for a full-time position should one come up in the future. Another teacher mentioned that students expect teachers to work hard so she didn't want to disappoint them. We need to value and care about the well-being of teachers (including students and staff).

WellAhead, funded by the McConnell Foundation, held a National Summit on Teacher and School Staff Well-being in 2017.

Participants reported that the rigidity of school systems makes it difficult to shift culture, structures, and behaviours to support workplace well-being.

Getting back to the set of questions above, I did all of those things for my whole career. The difference now is that I have adopted a mindset where I truly believe that self-care is important and my well-being is a priority.

So how do we find time to practice self-care when our plate is very full? First of all, keep self-care strategies simple. It just doesn't make sense to add to our workloads. This will just cause more stress, which defeats the purpose of implementing self-care strategies. Also, our self-care strategies need to be right for us at this particular time in our life. For example, I'm an empty-nester now so I have more time then I did 5 or 10 years ago when I had a full teaching load.

Finally, our self-care strategies should not be too hard, costly, or time-consuming. When I went back to teaching part-time, I knew that I needed to make some big changes to avoid burning out again. I was worried because I had developed several bad habits during my career. Although I had more time in my week because I was teaching less, I didn't want to add scheduled activities or expensive gym memberships. What I thought would work best for me would be to purposefully implement "new mindsets" and "new habits". In other words, I needed to abandon unhealthy mindsets and kick bad habits to the curb. The positive mindsets and new healthy habits would have to be achievable and increase my well-being.

Assess your level of self-care

I think it is useful to take some time to reflect and assess your current state of self-care, because there may be aspects of self-care that you haven't thought about. As a starting point, complete the self-care assessment below. This exercise has been adapted from two resources from Saakvitne & Pearlman and Skovholt & Trotter-Mathison.

When you are finished, look for patterns in your responses.

Add the date that you completed the assessment. Then set a reminder a month from now, three months from now, and six months from now to see if there are any positive changes.

SELF-CARE ASSESSMENT

Write down any self-care activities you engage in regularly.

It may be helpful to think about the different spheres of your life: physical, psychological, mental, emotional, spiritual and professional. What activities do you do that attend to self-care in each area?

For example,

Physical Self-Care

_ Do you eat meals regularly and maintain a healthy diet?

_ Do you see your doctor for preventative care?

Psychological Self-Care

_ Do you read something fun or interesting and unrelated to work

_ Do you get engaged in something interesting to you such as art, theater, or sports.

Emotional Self-Care

_ Spend time with people you enjoy

_ Do you stay in touch with important friends and family?

_ Do you practice self-compassion, forgive yourself, and even praise yourself for good deeds?

Spiritual Self-Care

_ Do you spend time in nature, even if it's a short walk or having a meal outside

_ Have you built a spiritual connection or community?

Relationship Self-Care

_ Do you make regular, scheduled date-nights with your spouse or partner?

_ Do you take time to reply to personal emails, and/or send holiday cards?

Professional Self-Care

_ Do you take a break during the workday, even if it's just lunch?

_ Do you set limits with co-workers and bosses?

These are not exhaustive. Feel free to activities and areas of self-care that are relevant for you.

Then Rate the following areas according to how often you do these things. Use different coloured highlighter pens so you can see the differences at-a-glance.

3 = frequently 2 = occasionally 1 = rarely 0 = I never do this

MY NEW MINDSETS

A MINDSET is an established set of attitudes. Like many people in my generation, I grew up in a household where my parents worked

very hard. My father was not home much because he was always working. When he was home and saw me, or my two sisters being idle, he would remark that there must be SOME-THING that we could be doing. My worldview is that one should always work hard and never be idle. I still fight this belief now even though I'm getting much better at allowing myself downtime. I talk to many teachers who were

also raised by very hard-working parents and have an incredible work ethic.

A mindset may be held by groups who adopt or accept behaviours or certain choices. Would you say that a teacher mindset may be one of working late, constant planning, and don't stop till you drop attitude? It is this "groupthink" as teachers that we have to let go off in order to be healthier and happier.

Teacher Behaviour

Teacher Beliefs, Myths and Mindsets

In a recent teacher self-care workshop, I asked teachers to discuss and list teacher beliefs, myths, and mindsets that contribute to teacher behaviour. I then asked how the beliefs, myths, and mindsets impact their ability to practice self-care.

Here are some of the beliefs they shared which can hurt them in the long run and lead to burnout:

* marking must be returned to students by the next class.
* all errors should be corrected (even though research suggests that this does not help students be better writers).
* teaching is about choosing between self-sacrifice and self-care.
* teachers need to answer questions even on a coffee break or during lunch, leaving no time to eat, drink, or use the bathroom.
* teachers must have all the answers.
* teachers never make mistakes.
* we must work now, and rest late.
* teachers don't take sick days.

We can't do away with mindsets altogether. What we can do is get rid of harmful beliefs and replace them with healthier mindsets. Here are some of the new mindsets I adopted.

Mindset 1: I Matter!

This was the most challenging mindset because for my entire career, I did not put myself first. I truly and strongly believe that I matter and people who love me think I matter too. While studying positive psychology, I came across a profound quote by Dr. Chris Peterson: "Other people matter." Peterson is one of the 100 most-cited psychologists in the world, one of the founding fathers of positive psychology including the impactful work of character strengths and virtues. When I read the quote, it made me reflect on its powerful message and that if other people matter, then I must matter too.

The activity below might help you achieve Mindset 1.

BEST POSSIBLE SELF ACTIVITY

This intervention was created by positive psychology Sonja Lyubomirsky and involves creating a detailed mental image of yourself at your best in all areas of your life—not just work. The purpose of this kind of positive intervention or activity is to cultivate a sense of optimism because it provides a buffer against negative health effects that you may be experiencing (e.g. stress, exhaustion, or burnout). Optimism provides us with a powerful feeling of the future. If you are struggling now at work, this is a simple but meaningful activity. This activity works best when combined with your self-care strategies.

Instructions:

Give yourself time and space to do this. The goal is to imagine yourself at some future date. It could be a month, six months, a year, or five years. The time period that you choose will be when you have fully implemented your self-care goals. Imagine how this feels for you and what your life looks like. You may write in a journal or in the form of a letter to your present self from this future self.

* Acknowledge and appreciate everything you did to get to where you are at this future point in your life.
* Allow your future self to express gratitude to the self who did (and will do) these things for you.
* Offer your present self words of compassion for overcoming your present challenges.
* Tell your present self the good that your future self sees in him/her, and the strengths (use your character strengths) that will help your present self become your future self.

Mindset 2: Guilt Be Gone!

Where does teacher guilt come from? When I think back to teacher mindsets, there is this invisible message that teachers must constantly do their best for their students (e.g. get that marking done, prepare outstanding lessons, be creative, and interesting while teaching). I am not advocating being lazy or slacking on your marking, but we should be able to have downtime without feeling guilty. It is not easy to let go of "teacher guilt" but the only way to do it is to keep referring back to Mindset 1.

Mindset 3: No more Badges of Honour

Teachers sometimes take pride in the stress and hard work of their job, treating it like a badge of honour. Wearing and comparing badges of honour is harmful to all teachers. Comments like "I marked 100 essays last night" or "I stayed up until 3 a.m. to get all my exams marked" are no longer part of my life. How did this notion of badges of honour become part of our teacher culture? More importantly, how do we break this unhealthy contest? Remember the quote "We cannot serve from an empty vessel" by Eleanor Brown. We cannot be our best when we are stressed, exhausted, and striving for unsustainable practices.

Mindset 4: Gratitude

One of the first things I did when I returned to my teaching job was to reflect on and list all of the things that I was grateful for because of that job. This helped me to stop being angry and blaming the institution for my burnout. It also made me look at the benefits of that career (e.g. income, learning opportunities, great colleagues). It was not my institution's fault that I choose the workloads and made decisions that were not good for me.

According to positive psychology research, being grateful, and expressing gratitude is the fastest way to increase one's well-being. The most common ways to do this is by writing in a gratitude journal.

THREE GOOD THINGS ACTIVITY

Each day, write down three good things that happened. I like to do this at night before I go to sleep. Even if we have had a tough day, there is always something to be grateful for!

However, I wanted to keep it simple, so in my case, I made a large mind map on a piece of flipchart paper with the name of the college where I worked in the centre. The idea was to think about all of the good that resulted from teaching there for 9 years instead of focusing on the negativity of leaving because of burnout. It was a great exercise because I came up with so many things that I was grateful for! If you want to share this activity with others, you could start a gratitude wall in your staff room.

Mindset 5: Let Go of Perfection

Discovering my character strengths had a huge impact on me. If you aren't familiar with this idea, more than 50 scientists spent about three years reviewing the best thinking on virtues and positive human qualities from theology psychology, and philosophy) from the past 2,500 years. The result was 24-character strengths which are universal across religions, cultures, nations, and belief systems. The VIA Character Strengths Survey is online and takes about 10 minutes. The survey asks you to evaluate 120 statements and say whether these statements match your habits or not. It asks about things like whether you finish tasks once you start them, whether you enjoy doing favors for friends, and whether you are good at coming up with original ideas or not.

The top 5-character strengths are our "signature" strengths or those that are most prevalent or used. My top character strength was Appreciation for Beauty and Excellence which made complete sense. Now the kicker. There is a downside if one over-uses a character strength, as you might expect. The overuse of Appreciation for Beauty and Excellence is *perfectionism*! When I saw that word, it was as if my whole teaching career flashed in front of me. I could agonize for hours over the right handout, test paper, or lesson plan. I had wasted so much valuable time when I could have used that time for me or my family. Sadly, many teachers tell me that they are perfectionists which means they create their own stress by holding themselves to impossible standards. Try the survey for free at http://www.viacharacter.org/www. Then complete the activity below.\

CHARACTER STRENGTHS FOR TEACHERS

Complete the VIA Character Strengths Survey and then list your top five-character strengths which are called Signature Strengths in the column on the left. In the column in the centre, write down how you use this strength as a teacher. In the column on the right, think of the downside of overusing this strength. (As I mentioned, for example, the shadow side of Appreciation of Beauty and Excellence is perfectionism). You can look at Michelle McQuaid's ebook How to Put Your Strengths to Work (https://www.michellemcquaid.com/product/how-to-put-your-strengths-to-work). to determine the shadow sides of each strength. You might be surprised how one of your strengths (and its overuse) is negatively impacting your life.

My Top 5 Character Strengths	How I use this strength as a teacher	How the overuse of this strengths affects me as a teacher

Reflection:

1. When are you at your best as a teacher?
2. What strengths help you to be your best as a teacher?
3. What positive impact do these strengths have on your students?
4. Is there a strength that you are not using now that could benefit you as a teacher?
5. Is there a strength that you could use in a new way? (research by Seligman, Steen, Park & Peterson, 2005 suggests that this makes us happier even in just one week!)

Mindset 6: Notice the Good Stuff

It's not always easy, but the more we focus on the positive things in life, the more positive we feel. Doing this also helps us feel gratitude, which as I've said, helps increase well-being. This mindset even applies to our students! Rather than complaining about problem students, we can choose to focus on the positive side of our students.

So, for example, I decided to have my EAP (English for Academic Purposes) students take the VIA Character Strengths Survey. I liked the idea of focusing on students' strengths instead of their weaknesses, because after years as an EAP instructor I felt that my job was becoming too much about pointing out errors or deficits in writing, with red pen in hand. And students are much more than their writing skills or their errors!

Here are two examples of how I was able to look for the good. I had a student who constantly challenged me in class. He always wanted to know why we had to do things a certain way or had questions about process. When I sat with this student to have him tell me what his top character strengths were, his number one strength was bravery! This put everything into context so instead of seeing the student as annoying, I saw him as having the courage to ask questions that no other students wanted to ask. Another student, who had hounded me via email for two weeks about making up a missed assignment, had fairness as his top strength. He felt that my denial of his request was unfair and that made sense to me, so we talked one day after class and I changed my mind about the make-up test.

Meeting forty students in one class requires time that we often do not have, but I wanted to be able to personally connect with each student. So I set up individual interviews with students after they completed the VIA Character Strengths Survey. During those interviews, I noticed two things. First, when I asked each student to tell me about their top five-character strengths and how they demonstrate them as a student, they immediately came to life! Normally in my EAP classes students are very quiet, but the same learners beamed and spoke with a sense of excitement as they talked about their strengths.

The second thing was a change in me. When I looked out at the sea of student's faces after the interviews, I saw their strengths instead of thinking about their writing skills. Character strengths such as curiosity, teamwork, leadership, kindness, and zest helped me to see these young people in a positive light.

Students had learned what they were good at and what was positive about themselves and so had I!

CHARACTER STRENGTHS FOR STUDENTS ACTIVITY

Noticing the good stuff as teachers is a sure way to increase our own well-being, but it also helps our students. Here is a mini-lesson plan on how to use the character strengths survey in class.

1. **Pre-writing activity**. First, we watched the video The Science of Strengths (https://www.youtube.com/watch?v=kq-rOelLciE) in class. Students discussed the content in small groups exploring such

questions as, "How are character strengths like super-powers?" and "What do you think your top strengths might be?"

2. **The survey**. The character strengths survey is free, takes about 10 minutes, and is available at http://www.viacharacter.org/www/Character-Strengths-Survey. I set up a free teacher account on the website with a designated link for the survey for each class. In this way I could get the survey results emailed to me and I could also verify that the students did actually complete the survey.

3. **Face-to-face interviews**. I set up a schedule with 10-minute time slots to talk to students about their top five-character strengths and how they use them specifically as a student. I created a form for this task which they were required to complete and bring to the interview. Reflecting on the survey results before the interview and being asked questions during the interview was part of a pre-writing exercise for their writing assignment.

4. **Writing assignment.** Students were required to write a 5-paragraph essay about their top three-character strengths. Although the top five are considered Signature Strengths (and the ones that are most easily and often used), choosing just three made it easier for the essay format.

Here are a few comments from the essays written by my students.

"In conclusion, identifying and building on your own unique character strengths can help make a better and happier person. I agree with the top three results of my VIA Character Strengths Survey (love, fairness, and kindness). Although I suppose I was aware of these traits, the survey made me stop and think about my character. In the future I will use these character strengths to bring out the best in me and help me to achieve the goals I set for my life. After all, it's what inside a person that counts."

"The three-character strengths of curiosity, love of learning, and leadership have aided me by providing me access to work opportunities, helping my performance in school, seek out learning opportunities, and increase the quality of my interpersonal relationships at school."

"My top three-character strengths are love, prudence and teamwork. I was not surprised to discover what they turned out to be. I would not even have changed the order in which they were given. It was reassuring to know what I thought I already knew."

Why Use Character Strengths?

There are many reasons why it could be a good idea, but I think the most important is that students should learn about their strengths and reflect on how they can use them (or how they have been using them in the past) to achieve results inside and outside of school. We know that our language learners can feel frustrated in their ability to learn English, so focusing on strengths could give them confidence. It is important to remember that all character strengths have downsides if overused, so that should be discussed as well. Overall, using our character strengths makes us feel happier, more confident, increases our energy, lessens our stress, helps us to achieve goals and grow as individuals. What teacher doesn't want that for his/her students?!

Mindset 7: "No" Is a Complete Sentence

How many times have you blurted out "yes" only to regret your decision later? I've lost track of the number of times that I have. It is ok to say no! If you are one of those teachers who cannot say no, trust me that if you do, the world will not open up and swallow you. Here's some great advice that buys you some time:

> When asked to do something, you can respond by saying "Thank you for the opportunity. I'm not sure I can do this now. Let me get back to you in a few days." By doing this, you are giving yourself time to make a wise decision and more importantly, preparing the person that you may say no.

Mindset 8: Teaching Is a Career, Not a Lifestyle

The bottom line is that I deserve a personal life and so do you! I remind myself that time is nonrefundable and that teaching will expand to fill whatever time I give it.

If you are not ready to embrace new mindsets, then it will be very difficult to practice self-care. Feel free to use or adapt any of my new mindsets. Or design your own set of mindsets that will work for you.

NEW HEALTHY HABITS

"The only proper way to eliminate bad habits is to replace them with good ones"
—Jerome Hines.

THINK ABOUT some of your current habits, good or bad. Habits are an acquired mode of behaviour that has become nearly or completely involuntary, like brushing our teeth before we go to bed. What habits could be getting in the way of our self-care?

My goal was to replace some bad habit such as drinking too much coffee with good habits like drinking more water. Here's my list of new habits:

Habit 1: Walk!

I've never been a gym person so getting more movement into my day had to happen naturally. I love to walk so I decided to save money and forego a parking pass. This meant a 20-30-minute walk to the school three times a week. I was able to save money and get exercise, so it worked perfectly for me. The other benefit was that I had time to think about my lesson before I got to class and then reflect on what went well on the way back to the car. I think as teachers we often don't have time to reflect because of our busy lives. Research suggests that being outside every day for even as little as 5 minutes can significantly improve our mood. (Ryan et al, 2014).

Habit 2: Set Reasonable Marking Expectations

I wish that this was something that I did many years ago. One beautiful May day, I thought I should sit on my deck and mark papers. Then I decided that I really didn't want to, so I spent my day off in the garden. When I went to class the next day, I told students that I did not have their papers marked and guess what happened?

Absolutely nothing!

All those years of stressing over marking and it appeared that the pressure to get it done was coming from me, not from the students. Lesson learned!

Habit 3: Minimalist Marking

This relates to Habit 2 and expectations of marking. I know some teachers who correct every error on a paper. There is research to support that this does not actually make students better writers. I never adopted that practice of correcting everything, but I have seen some interesting posts on social media about minimalist marketing, meaning deciding what specific errors will be marked or giving students editing symbols so they have to find their own errors. It makes sense to do this especially with many writing classes at colleges having 50 or more students.

Habit 4: No Email on Weekends or Evenings

Let students know when you will answer emails and when you won't. And stick to your schedule. Again, students seemed to be fine with the schedule I set for returning email. No screams, no noise, nothing.

Habit 5: Drink More Water and Less Coffee

Spending $4 several times a week on a good coffee is nice, but I wanted to work less and stress less about income. It was an easy switch from a coffee cup to a water bottle. Less caffeine just makes sense.

Habit 6: Avoid the "Moan Zone"

Do you have a staff room at your school that is filled with nothing but negativity and complaints? It can be contagious, so I stay clear! In fact, research suggests that venting can lead to increased negative emotions and higher risk of burnout (WellAhead, 2018). The antidote to moaning is to express something "good" to a colleague. For example, you could say "I really liked it when …" or "You are so good at …" Don't forget to include the hard-working admin staff and your students! One way to keep a positive attitude is the **Best Possible Self Activity** at the end of the book.

Habit 7: After-work Ritual

Dr. Adam Fraser talks about "the third space" which gives you time to mentally transition from work life to home life. It's not necessarily a physical area but a way to "power down" from your day. (Fraser, 2012). My ritual is as follows: I drop my bag off at the front door and go to the kitchen to make a cup of decaf tea. I decompress by watching a rerun of *CSI Las Vegas*. After a break, I'm ready to tackle chores, cooking, and so on.

Habit 8: Spend Time Doing Things I Like Other Than Teaching

I used to spend most of my free time working or reading about teaching English. Now I make sure that I plan activities that bring me joy.

Habit 9: Connect With People Important to Me!

Most of my friends are teachers and they are great people, but I think it's good to connect with people during our personal time that are not teachers. You can learn a lot from people who do other kinds of work. I make sure I schedule coffee/lunch with friends who I value.

Habit 10: Have a Non-work Day

Teachers must switch off and de-stress sometimes. It's just that simple. The hard part is that is it is difficult for us to unwind at the end of the day since our profession involves active involvement such as planning and marking. We often end up doing work on the weekends as well. It never ends until the course or semester is over. But it's important to have at least one day a week where you don't work.

It is also important to give our voice a rest. Almost 20% of teachers in the US reported missed work due to voice disorders (Acoustica Society of America, 2015). I actually met a Canadian teacher at the Teacher Self-Care Conference in Atlanta who completely lost her voice and was on leave for a year.

How Do Other Teachers Practice Self-Care?

In the past few years, I have interviewed many teachers from around the world. One specific question that I ask is about their self-care practices. Here are some responses:

> *"In my spare time, I am a musician. I remember what a professor once told me in my days as an undergraduate. She said, 'Find a hobby or recreation you truly love to do outside of teaching. This will help keep you centered and you won't burn yourself out.' I have taken this to heart." —**Jose Torres, USA***

Reading would be my number one answer. I love surfing You-Tube and Netflix, listening to music, and playing with my kids to help me unwind. Whenever I can, a lovely drive through the mountains rejuvenates me always! —**Suzanne Rajkumar, Honduras**

Cooking, reading, and exercising are the best ways for me to relax on a normal day. In fact, they're so important that I schedule them into my calendar along with 15-30 minutes of time for coffee (without work) in the morning. If it's on my calendar, it gets done. During the year, I've also made it a priority to schedule in longer breaks in so I can get a full week or two to shut off. This time away usually leads to my best 'brain work' or strategy planning. —**Annemarie Fowler, USA**

I spend as much time with my wife and daughters as I can, play the guitar, and read. I try to get to the beach or down to the park as often as I can. —**Nik Peachey, UK**

Spending time with my family and friends, reading and writing, attending cultural events such as concerts and language exchanges, having a coffee, and a good conversation. ~**Lina Marcela Gómez Quintero, Colombia**

I enjoy playing guitar, cycling, hiking in nature, doing yoga, flying my drone, hanging out with friends, reading, meditating, and among other things...just chilling at home. —**Brad Deacon, Japan**

I like exercising, especially walking, and yoga. I also connect with friends via phone or online chats. After working on my computer, it's refreshing to switch gears and be involved in experiences that use tactile and kinesthetic senses, such as cooking and dancing. —**Julie Vorholt, USA**

SELF-CARE FOR ONLINE TEACHERS

IN MY self-care workshops and presentations for teachers, I realized I have left out a group—online teachers. Given the interest and growth in online learning, it goes without saying that the demand for instructors will increase as well. This is good news for teachers who make a living from online instruction. However, this form of teaching takes place in front of a screen while sitting for long periods. There is a body of research that has found a correlation between long periods of sitting and elevated risk of illness or injury. How can self-care strategies be used to be healthier as online instructors?

Although I'm not teaching English online, I do spend most of my day writing and coaching teachers online. I sit for several hours a day, but I do try to take regular breaks. For example, I used to fill a pitcher of water and keep it on my desk to ensure I drank enough during the day. I now use a glass which means that I have to get up frequently to re-fill it.

I believe that self-care strategies for all teachers should be easy to do, no-cost/low-cost (state-of-the-art standing desks are not in everyone's budget) and not add time to our already very busy work schedule.

Before you get started on determining the self-care strategies that work best for you, use a free sitting time calculator to find out how much you sit each day. There's one at https://www.movemoresitless. org.au/sitting-calculator.

Here are some simple self-care strategies for sitting teachers:

1. Alternate between sitting and standing every 30 minutes.

Standing more can increase your energy and productivity levels, lower your stress, and improve your mood.

2. Incorporate some simple exercises in both seated and standing positions. Standing more can boost your metabolism, tone muscles, and even reduce common aches and pains.

3. Stand when appropriate. For example, I had a WhatsApp call the other day with someone who was in Barbados. While she walked outside amongst the palm trees, I propped my phone up on a book shelf and stood and stretched.

4. If you live in a flat, take the stairs. (I take the stairs daily when I collect the mail in the lobby of my apartment building).

5. Plan for a midday exercise class or walk. Research suggests that even 5 minutes outside will significantly improve our mood. (Ryan et al, 2014).

6. Set an alarm to remind you to take breaks.

7. Design your own standing desk by stacking books or using a small table. Remember your monitor needs to be at eye level, and make sure that whatever you put on your desk is stable.

8. Instead of sitting on a chair, use a physio-ball. This way you're using your core muscles even while you're sitting and your posture will be better than if you were sitting on a regular chair.

When Your Office Is Your Home

Teaching online from home requires some other self-care strategies to avoid exhaustion or burnout. When one's workplace and home are in the same location, this creates certain challenges. If possible, it's important to have a place "just for teaching" which is separate from the rest of your home.

Have an end-of-the-day ritual which gives you time to mentally transition from work life to home life. Since your home and your work are in the same area, it's helpful to have a way to "power down" from your day.

ORGANIZATIONAL STRATEGIES

A SUPPORTIVE professional culture is imperative for teacher well-being. To create this kind of positive environment, there must be respect, a feeling of belonging, acceptance, opportunities for professional learning and sharing among colleagues (Carney, 2015).

When I first started presenting on teacher self-care, my workshops focused on what teachers can do but a teacher asked an interesting question during a presentation that made me think differently. She asked, "Why must the onus be on teachers to do everything? We already do so much now. Telling us that we need to care about our own self-care is just one more responsibility given to us."

It's a great question that isn't often answered in the research. When I first started reading about teacher self-care, I believed that it was our responsibility to make good decisions and plan rejuvenating activities for our self-care. I have shifted my thinking based on examples of best practices in countries like Australia and England where "wellness committees" are being formed in schools. Peer mentoring, mental health training, workplace health policies, and/or workplace wellness programs are some organization-level interventions that can be implemented. Mindfulness programs are also becoming more popular for teachers with great stress-reducing benefits (Abenavoli, Harris, Katz, Jennings, Greenberg, 2013). As teachers, do we have a vital role to play in terms of saying no, scheduling "me time", setting reasonable marking expectations, and getting enough sleep but there are often things outside our control that we cannot change. Administrators must also be responsible for creating an environment where teachers feel supported and where reasonable workloads are given.

- What support doesn't look like:Criticizing teachers or tolerating teachers who openly criticize each other
- Allowing teachers to brag about how early they come to school
- Creating a culture of competition instead of cooperation
- Expecting teachers to always take on more and more work
- Contacting teachers after-hours and on weekends

Specific Strategies for Administrators

In 2016, Robert Half, a staffing firm, asked Canadians what drives their happiness at work? No, it's not salary. The top three responses given by employees were:

a. Feeling pride in their organization
b. Being appreciated for the work that they do
c. Being treated with fairness and respect

Real appreciation and meaningful praise creatives a positive work environment, conveys respect and increase our well-being (for both the giver and receiver). It's a win-win situation (Gillespie & McGibbon).

These findings align with feedback gathered from a teacher self-care webinar that I hosted. Teachers indicated that a good work environment and feeling valued, respected, appreciated for their work contributed to their well-being. Being appreciated for a job well done is a simple, free, but powerful way to support teachers!

For many new teachers, the first year or two is demanding and creates anxiety. Some beginning teachers noted that workloads, physical tiredness, voice problems, negative school culture, isolation, inadequate time for eating and toilet breaks and emotional tiredness impacted their well-being (McCallum & Price, 2010). Think back to your own career. Would it have been helpful to have a mentor or self-care training? For new teachers, stress levels are extremely high so buddies or mentors are a good way to provide support.

The Environment

It is also imperative that teachers be provided with proper workspaces. A friend of mine who is a college faculty indicated that personal desks were recently removed and replaced by open-concept shared computer stations. Teachers share a space, if one is available. They can no longer speak to students in private. I find this appalling and disrespectful. Webinar participants who work in these open-concept areas explained:

"One day I went to work and had no desk at all."

"There is very little workspace and rooms are over-crowded with colleagues talking all the time while you are trying to work"

Administrators, teachers are your greatest resource. What are you doing to facilitate their health and well-being? Are you asking staff how they are by checking in on a regular basis? Are you providing the Maslach Burn out inventory for teachers to assess their level of well-being? And, leaders, do not forget to take care of your own well-being!

I'm excited to read how the workplace wellness literature and school staff wellness is coming together to improve the well-being of all staff. It is important to note two things here: 1) teachers are often reluctant to engage in well-being initiatives for fear of judgement and being seen as "not coping well" and 2) well-being initiatives be relevant and not add to teacher workload adding additional stress (WellAhead, 2018). My desire is to see an increase in the recognition and importance of well-being and the dedication of time and resources to supporting wellness for all.

Yes, teachers have a full-plate and ideally, all schools should embrace flourishing and well-being but we shouldn't wait. (Cherkowski & Walker, 2018).

What support looks like…

I saw a Twitter post online that provided an example of how educational leaders can support teacher well-being. The message, in the form of an automatic email reply, looked something like this:

> Thank you for your email. As part of our school's commitment to well-being, our staff are not expected to read or answer emails sent after 6 p.m. during the week or during the weekend/holidays. If you do not receive a reply, the teacher is not being rude but choosing his/her well-being in order to be the best possible teacher.

SELF-CARE REFLECTION

1. Thinking about yellow lights, answer the following two questions for yourself. You may want to brainstorm answers with some of your colleagues. What is one thing that you can stop doing immediately as a form of self-care that does not cost money or take more of your time?

   Can't think of anything? Here are some ideas from webinar participants:

   - thinking about next semester
   - staying up late
   - trying to be perfect
   - overthinking
   - going to work early and staying late
   - reading work emails on my phone at home
   - allowing school to take over my home life

2. What is one thing that you can start doing immediately as a form of self-care that does not cost money or take more of your time?

   Stuck? Here are some more great ideas from workshop participants:

   - taking strength breaks
   - having a sense of humour
   - smiling
   - taking vacation days

- encouraging and supporting co-workers
- having more fun
- using a timer: Here's how it works: After you finish teaching, go to your desk to plan/mark and set a timer with a reasonable amount of time. When it goes off, stop what you are doing, and leave work. It's simple and it works.

FINAL WORDS

I HAVE learned several things along this journey of burnout and back to the classroom. The key for me was the need for a radical change in my teacher mindset. I refuse to wear "badges of honour" because it is not healthy. Time is precious and I matter to me and the people who love me. Being older and wiser, what would I tell my younger teacher self?

* It's ok to put myself first. You are allowed to have a personal life.
* Obsess less. Perfection is not the goal— No one is perfect.
* Be kind to myself—Teaching skills develops over time.
* Say no—The world won't open up and swallow me! (Teaching will expand to fill whatever time you give it)
* Set reasonable expectations for marking.

When I prepared my first presentation on teacher self-care, I was anxious about telling my story of burnout. I remember telling the audience what I lost: income, seniority, pension earnings, connections with colleagues, and a career that I loved. More importantly, there are many things that I gained from leaving the profession for 18 months. I became healthier, happier, and understood the importance of self-care for my own well-being.

If you have to take time off, then do so. Do not feel guilty. You need to do what is best for you. Sometimes the only way to get better is to leave the classroom. Our health and well-being are so important and they should never be compromised.

Research conducted in the field of positive psychology by Roepke & Seligman (2015) suggests that people who see new opportunities after a challenging life event, benefit-finding or by seeing "doors opening" can grow. We cannot change a stressful or challenging life event but we can change the way we think about it. This gives us personal power and the ability to grow. When I reflect now, professional burnout gave me time off to study positive psychology, which helps me now in my career.

Others have reported that adversity resulted in some positive results such as:

1. My eyes opened to paths I hadn't seen before
2. My interactions with people showed me interesting new opportunities
3. It seemed like "when one door closes, another door opens"
4. I saw new ways to help people
5. I found a new inspiration
6. I found a new source of meaning in life

I believe that I have gained perspective and insight, developed new skills and re-invented myself (teacher to teacherpreneur and workshops and numerous presentations including keynote and plenary speaking locally and internationally) because I left classroom teaching. It doesn't mean we have to leave teaching forever, but you may see doors opening for you if you do leave. Using the car analogy, we understand the importance of our vehicle having regular maintenance in order to keep it running well. As teachers, we must also commit to regular maintenance or self-care so we are able to balance the demands of our profession and give what is best in us, not what is left in us.

DISCUSSION QUESTIONS FOR BOOK CLUB

SHARING OUR thoughts and ideas from any book can be insightful and interesting. Think about how organizing a "book-club" discussion can further support teacher self-care. I have provided some questions to get you started.

1. What stood out for you from the book?
2. What are specific ways that you practice self-care now?
3. How can the image of the traffic signals guide us in increasing our well-being and taking time for our own self-care?
4. What are some teacher beliefs, mindsets, and myths that influence teacher behaviour and result in bad habits? Where do we learn these things? How can we challenge them? How can they impact are self-care?
5. How can we support each other to ensure self-care practices? (individually, interpersonally, and at an organizational level)
6. Would the formation of a well-being committee facilitate teacher well-being and self-care practices at your school? How can this be done?
7. Would surveying faculty be a useful way to gather feedback on the current state of teacher ill-being or well-being?

Best Possible Self Activity

This intervention was created by positive psychology Sonja Lyubomirsky and involves creating a detailed mental image of yourself at your best in all areas of your life—not just work. The purpose of this kind of positive intervention or activity is to cultivate a sense of optimism because it provides a buffer against negative health effects that you may be experiencing (e.g. stress, exhaustion, or burnout). Optimism provides us with a powerful feeling of the future. If you are struggling now at work, this is a simple but meaningful activity. This activity works best when combined with your self-care strategies. You can do it alone or make it part of a professional development book club by sharing your reflections with others. Support each other by giving praise, gratitude, and constructive advice.

Instructions:

Give yourself time and space to do this. The goal is to imagine yourself at some future date. It could be a month, six months, a year, or five years. The time period that you choose will be when you have fully implemented your self-care goals. Imagine how this feels for you and what your life looks like. You may write in a journal or in the form of a letter to your present self from this future self.

Here are some guidelines:
- Acknowledge and appreciate everything you did to get to where you are at this future point in your life.
- Allow your future self to express gratitude to the self who did (and will do) these things for you.
- Offer your present self words of compassionate for overcoming your present challenges.
- Tell your present self the good that your future self sees in him/her, and the strengths (use your character strengths) that will help your present self become your future self.

BIBLIOGRAPHY

Acton, R., & Glasgow, P. (2015). Teacher wellbeing in neoliberal contexts: A review of the literature. *Australian Journal of Teacher Education, 40(8)*, 99-114. http://dx.doi.org/10.14221/ajte.2015v40n8.6/

Abenavoli, R., Jennings, P., Harris, A., Katz, D., Greenberg, M. (2013). The protective effects of mindfulness against burnout among educators. *The Psychology of Education Review, 37(2)*, 57-69

Access Alliance. (n.d.). Good Jobs Campaign. Retrieved from https://accessalliance.ca/pathways-to-economic-security/good-jobs-campaign/

Barnett, J. E. and Cooper, N. (2009). Creating a culture of self-care. *Clinical Psychology: Science and Practice, 16*, 16-20. doi:10.1111/j.1468-2850.2009.01138.x

Carney, P. (2015). *Well aware: Developing resilient, active, and flourishing students*. Toronto: Pearson Canada.

Cherkowski, S. & Walker, K. (2018). *Teacher wellbeing. Noticing, nurturing, sustaining and flourishing in schools*. Ontario: Word & Deed Publishing.

TEDx Talks. (2016, April 15). *Amy Cunningham, Drowning in Empathy: The Cost of Vicarious Trauma*. [Video file]. Retrieved from https://www.youtube.com/watch?v=ZsaorjIo1Yc

Curry, J. R. P., & O'Brien, E. R. P. (2012). Shifting to a wellness paradigm in teacher education: A promising practice for fostering teacher stress reduction, burnout resilience, and promoting retention. *Ethical Human Psychology and Psychiatry, 14(3)*, 178-191.

Emmons, R.A., & McCullough, M.E. (2003). Counting blessings versus burdens: an experimental investigation of gratitude and subjective well-being in daily life. *Journal of Personality and Social Psychology, 84(2)*, 377-89.

Fraser, A. (2012*). The third space: Using life's little transitions to find balance and happiness* [Kindle]. Retrieved from Amazon.com

Gillespie, K., & McGibbon, A. (2018, October 18). The Next Collection of Well-being Insights: October 2018. [online newsletter]. Retrieved from https://fowinsights.com/insights/culture/collection-wellbeing-insights-part-2/.

Higher Education Academy Research Briefing. (2013*). The importance of emotional resilience for staff and students in the 'helping' professions: Developing an emotional curriculum.* University of Bedfordshire: Grant, L. & Kinman, G. Available from https://www.heacademy.ac.uk/system/files/emotional_resilience_louise_grant_march_2014_0.pdf

Holmes, E. (2005). *Teacher well-being: Looking after yourself and your career in the classroom.* London: Routledge Falmer.

Howell, C. (2016). Listening, learning, caring & counselling: The essential manual for psychologists, psychiatrists, counsellors & other healthcare professionals on caring for their clients. Exisle Publishing Pty.

CPRE. (2014). *Seven trends: The transformation of the teaching force, updated April 2014.* (#RR-80). Consortium for Policy Research in Education, University of Pennsylvania: Ingersoll, R., Merrill, L., & Stuckey, D. Available at https://cpre.org/sites/default/files/workingpapers/1506_7trendsapril2014.pdf.

IRIS Connect UK. (2018). Improving teacher happiness and well-being. A collection of expert resources. Available from https://discover.irisconnect.com/teacher-happiness-and-wellbeing

Johnson, S., Cooper, C., Cartwright, S., Donald, I., Taylor P. & Millet, C. (2005). The experience of work-related stress across occupations. *Journal of Managerial Psychology, 20(2).* 178-187 https://www.emeraldinsight.com/doi/abs/10.1108/02683940510579803.

Knowledge Sourcing Intelligence LLP. (January 2018). *Global Online Education Market - Forecasts from 2018 to 2023.* Dublin, Ireland.

Klusmann, U., Richter, D., & Lüdtke, O. (2016). Teachers' emotional exhaustion is negatively related to students' achievement: Evidence from a large-scale assessment study. *Journal of Educational Psychology, 108(8)*, 1193-1203. https://eric.ed.gov/?id=EJ1119100/

McCallum, F., & Price, D. (2010). Well teachers, well students. *Journal of Student Well-being, 4(1)*, 19–34. DOI: 10.21913/JSW.v4i1.599

Maslach, C., Schaufeli, W. B., & Leiter, M. P. (2001). Job burnout. *Annual Review of Psychology, 52(1)*, 397-422. https://doi.org/10.1146/annurev.psych.52.1.397

Newell, J & MacNeil, G. (2010). Professional burnout, vicarious trauma, secondary traumatic stress, and compassion fatigue: A review of theoretical terms, risk factors, and preventive methods for clinicians and researchers. *Best Practices in Mental Health, 6 (2)*, 57-68 Available at https://pdfs.semanticscholar.org/37aa/59deafaca84 5ce22843d398310df14fbf576.pdf/

WellAhead (2017*) National Summit on Teacher and School Staff Well-being: Summary Report + Next Steps.* Retrieved from https://static1.squarespace.com/static/586814ae2e69cfb1676a5c0b/t/5a5c c667e4966b7d9b0cff8e/1516029547042/Staff+Wellbeing+Summit_Summary+FINAL+WellAhead.pdf

WellAhead (2018) *Research Brief: Promoting the Well-being of Teachers and School Staff.* Retrieved from https://static1.squarespace.com/static/586814ae2e69cfb1676a5c0b/t/5b281bb170a 6ad31c89ab315/1529355185939/TSWB_ResearchBrief.pdf

Robert Half International Inc. (2016). *The secrets of the happiest companies and employees.* Menlo Park, CA: Todd Henry and Daniel Pink. Downloaded from https://www.roberthalf.com/its-time-we-all-work-happy.

Roepke, A. M., & Seligman, M. E. (2015). Doors opening: A mechanism for growth after adversity. *The Journal of Positive Psychology, 10(2)*, 107-115. DOI: 10.1080/17439760.2014.913669

Ryan, R., Weinstein, N., Bernstein, J., Warren Brown, K, Mistretta, L., Gagné, M. (2010) Vitalizing effects of being outdoors and in nature. *Journal of Environmental Psychology, 30 (2)*, 159. DOI: 10.1016/j.jenvp.2009.10.009

Seligman, M. E. P., Steen, T. A., Park, N., & Peterson, C. (2005). Positive psychology progress: Empirical validation of interventions. *American Psychologist, 60(5)*, 410-421.http://dx.doi.org/10.1037/0003-066X.60.5.410

Sheldon, K. M., & Lyubomirsky, S. (2006). How to increase and sustain positive emotion: The effects of expressing gratitude and visualizing best possible selves. *Journal of Positive Psychology, 1(2)*, 73-82.

Skovholt, T. M., & Trotter-Mathison, M. (2016). *The resilient practitioner: Burnout and compassion fatigue prevention and self-care strategies for the helping professions.* Abingdon: Routledge.

Skovholt, T. M., & D'Rozario, V. (2000). Portraits of outstanding and inadequate teachers in Singapore: The impact of emotional intelligence. *Teaching and Learning, 21(1)*, 9-17.

Soini, T., Pyhältö, K., & Pietarinen, J. (2010). Pedagogical well-being: Reflecting learning and well-being in teachers' work. *Teachers and Teaching, 16(6)*, 735-751, DOI: 10.1080/13540602.2010.517690

Split, J. L., Koomen, H.M. & Thijs, J.T. (2011). Teacher well-being: The importance of teacher-student relationships. *Educational Psychology Review, 23(4)*, 457–477. DOI https://doi.org/10.1007/s10648-011-9170-y

Spurgeon, J & Thompson, L. (2018). Rooted in Resilience: A Framework for the Integration of Well-Being in Teacher Education Programs. Master of Applied Positive Psychology (MAPP) Capstone Projects, University of Pennsylvania, 144. https://repository.upenn.edu/mapp_capstone/144

Stanley, J. (2014, October 13). How unsustainable workloads are destroying the quality of teaching. *Schools Week.* Retrieved from https://schoolsweek.co.uk/how-unsustainable-workloads-are-destroying-the-quality-of-teaching/

Stoeber, J., & Rennert, D. (2008). Perfectionism in school teachers: Relations with stress appraisals, coping styles, and burnout. *Anxiety, Stress, & Coping, 21(1)*, 37-53. DOI: 10.1080/10615800701742461

The Varkey Foundation. (2018). *Global Teacher Status Index 2018.* London: Dolton P., Marcenaro, O., De Vries, R., She P. Available at https://www.varkeyfoundation.org/media/4790/gts-index-9-11-2018.pdf

Whiting, J. K., Jensen, Z. R., Leishman, T.W., Beradi, M. L, & Hunter, E. J. (2015) Classroom acoustics for vocal health of elementary school teachers. In *Proceedings from Meetings on Acoustics 23(1).* Acoustical Society of America.

ABOUT THE AUTHOR

AFTER 20 years in the ESL classroom, I have made the successful transition to teacherpreneur. A teacherpreneur is an educator who combines his/her creativity, skills and expertise to develop products, resources and/or services for additional income. In short, I make a living doing the things that I love: designing courses and teaching materials, facilitating workshops, and presenting at conferences. And writing books like the one you are holding in your hands right now.

As a teacher, I have taught students from 8 to 80 years in a variety of educational environments such as English for Specific Purposes (ESP), English for Academic Purposes (EAP), Business English, and taught communication courses at post-secondary institutions. During my 7 years in Hong Kong, I was responsible for developing English Language curricula for secondary schools, vocational training programs and summer intensive courses. I also developed and delivered workshops for teachers of English related to teaching and learning.

I have a Master of Education degree in Teaching, Learning and Development from Brock University, Canada; a Master of Arts degree from the Ontario Institute for Studies in Education (OISE) of the University of Toronto and a Bachelor of Arts degree from York University, Canada. I am TESL Ontario certified (OCELT) and accredited as a TESL Trainer for Methodology and Theory; Practicum Supervisor and Academic Coordinator.

I have certificates in Positive Psychology and Positive Education from Wilfred Laurier University in Canada as well as a coaching credential with the Centre for Positive Psychology in the USA. I recently completed SmartEducation™ SMART: Stress Management and Resiliency Techniques for Educators which is an evidence-based program offered by the University of British Columbia. The goal is to help educators cultivate mindfulness, self-compassion, optimism and self-care and I hope to introduce what I have learned in upcoming trainings. In the last few years, I have given more than 25 workshops, presentations and keynotes speeches on teacher well-being and self-care and continue to share what I have learned from my own personal experience and from speaking with other teachers both locally and internationally.

Connect with me

If you have any questions about this book or are interested in a keynote speaker or presentation. Please contact me at palmer.patrice@gmail.com. Or find me on Twitter (@positiveupside), LinkedIn at https://www.linkedin.com/in/patricepalmer1/ and Instagram, (@educatorwellbeing).

For additional resources on well-being and more about what I do, please visit my website, www.patricepalmer.ca.